Also written By Elly Valas: *Guerrilla Retailing*

Also written by Mark Mayberry: *Building the Dream Workforce*

Lessons from the Links

Managing Business Like the Pros

**Elly Valas
and
Mark Mayberry**

iUniverse, Inc.
Bloomington

Lessons from the Links
Managing Business Like the Pros

iUniverse books may be ordered through booksellers or by contacting:

iUniverse
1663 Liberty Drive
Bloomington, IN 47403
www.iuniverse.com
1-800-Authors (1-800-288-4677)

Because of the dynamic nature of the Internet, any web addresses or links contained in this book may have changed since publication and may no longer be valid. The views expressed in this work are solely those of the author and do not necessarily reflect the views of the publisher, and the publisher hereby disclaims any responsibility for them.

ISBN: 978-1-4502-7634-4 (sc)
ISBN: 978-1-4502-7636-8 (dj)
ISBN: 978-1-4502-7635-1 (ebk)

Printed in the United States of America

iUniverse rev. date: 2/4/2011

Dedications

To my mom, who always made me feel so special; to Lynn, who has brought such joy to my life; and to Elly, who is an incredible friend and has been the driving force behind this book.
—*Mark Mayberry*

To Ruben, Aaron, Rachel, Josh, Kyla, and Ari, who keep me young and add so much to my life; to David, Claudia, and Leslie; to Sandy and Ada who are always there for me; and to all those who continue to golf with me no matter how little I practice; thank you for your patience.
—*Elly Valas*

Contents

Preface

I will be forever grateful to Barry Gunn, owner of Edmonds and Y. Franks, the Appliance Stores, in Burnaby, BC, for taking a discussion during a NARDA board meeting completely off course with his comment: "I manage my business the same way I play golf." Barry is an excellent golfer, but I needed to know more about his comparison of the game to his retail stores.

That single idea became the seed for much thought and for this book.

Golf is a singular game—just the player against the course, the conditions, and his or her own strengths and weaknesses.

Similarly, business is a singular endeavor—just the owner or manager against the competition, market conditions, and the strengths and weaknesses of the businesses.

On our next golf outing, I shared Barry's idea with my friend Mark Mayberry. Mark was a successful businessman himself, and during the entire round we looked for—and found—similarities between business management and golf.

By the time we got back to the clubhouse, we had the framework for this book in mind—two golfers talking about what matters most as they rode around a tree-lined, hazard-filled course.

This is for all those who "tee off" every day in the great game of business.

—*Elly Valas*

Making the Date

"I still can't believe Bill and Dick didn't show up this morning!"

Making the Date

"Not another one! We can't keep losing customers like this!" Matt was fuming as he slammed the phone down. "Nobody's getting a thing done around here, and I'm wasting all *my* time putting out fires."

Already frustrated about losing a bid to a competitor and listening to two of his associates bicker over a commission, this latest news hit Matt like a rock.

"What's going on around here?" Matt yelled. "Doesn't anyone care? I'm working harder than ever and we're just sliding."

Matt was exhausted. After he had spent years as a successful business owner, things had turned sour. He was burned out, and it seemed like nothing he tried helped turn his business around. "It just never ends," he sighed. "I've owned this company for a long time, and we've been successful through the years; but right now, the wheels are coming off."

Matt picked up his coffee cup and walked to the window, looking across the cityscape. "I wonder how Elizabeth does it," Matt thought as he saw the top of her office building across town. "I know her business is as competitive as ours, but she seems to have all the luck. I never hear her complain, and her business is growing like crazy. Hmmmm. Maybe she could help me."

With that, he picked up the phone.

"Elizabeth Bailey," she answered. Elizabeth's voice reflected her smile. It was strong and confident. She greeted Matt warmly, asking how things were going.

"I'm not having much fun right now."

"I'm sorry to hear it. What's going on?"

"I don't really know. I can't put my finger on it, but things here just seem to be falling apart."

"Like what?"

"Like everything. Our service level has dropped, and we're getting more complaints; I can't get a handle on my inventory, and I've had more staff turnover than I can ever remember."

"Sounds tough, Matt."

"Yeah. I've had two new competitors open up in this area. They're getting all the new accounts, and I hear that their businesses are growing like crazy. There doesn't seem to be any customer loyalty anymore. Some of my best customers don't think twice about our relationship when these new guys call them. Our history together doesn't seem to mean anything. Our sales and profits are slipping too."

"That's not too surprising with all the other stuff you're going through. Is there anything I can do to help?"

"Actually, Elizabeth, that's why I called. I was hoping I could come out and pick your brain over a cup of coffee. You just seem to be doing everything right, and I could use some ideas."

Elizabeth giggled as she sloughed off Matt's compliment. "I don't know about *everything*, but I'm happy to try to give you a hand. I'll tell you what, Matt; I'm looking for an excuse to go play golf next week. Will Thursday work?"

"Golf! I haven't had time to play in months. As a matter of fact, I think the last time I picked up a club was when you and I played at that new course north of town."

"That's all the more reason to get out. I've learned some of the most important business lessons on the golf course, Matt. It's the perfect place to talk about what you're up against."

"What does golf have to do with business?" Matt asked.

"Well, if businesspeople ran their businesses the way the pros play golf, they would all be doing better. Golfers like Arnold Palmer, Jack Nicklaus, and Phil Mickelson don't change their games based on their pairings or who tops the leader board. Their game play is based on the conditions of the course and their own strengths. They work to overcome their weaknesses and are constantly trying to improve, but they do what works for them, not what others on the tour might be doing."

"Hmmm … sounds like an interesting idea. And maybe getting out of the office for a while will give me some new perspective."

"Okay. I've got a couple of things to get done first thing that morning, but why don't you pick me up at my office at ten? You get us a tee time and we'll have a chance to talk."

"I really appreciate the help, Elizabeth. I just don't know what to do. I feel sort of like I did when I first started in this business nineteen years ago. I'll let you go now, and we'll talk more when we play."

It All Starts at the Bag Drop

"There is a golf God!"

It All Starts at the Bag Drop

Matt pulled into the golf course's parking lot and stopped at the bag drop. A smiling, smartly dressed bag boy greeted them.

"Hi there! I'm Sam. Let me get your bags for you. Is this your first time here?"

"Yes," Matt said.

"Matt and I have heard great things about the course," Elizabeth told Sam.

"It's a terrific course," said Sam. "And we try to deliver great service. We want you to come back and to tell your friends about us too." Looking at the tag on Matt's bag, Sam said, "I know that your name is Matt." Turning to Elizabeth, he asked, "What's yours?"

"I'm Elizabeth. Nice to meet you, Sam."

"What name is the tee time under, and what time is it for?"

"The tee time is under my name: Jennings," said Matt. "It's for 11:22."

"Great," Sam said. "You can park your car right over there and head for the pro shop. They're expecting you. You have about thirty minutes before you tee off, so you'll have time to try our practice range if you want. After you check in, walk down these stairs and your clubs will be on your cart."

Elizabeth tipped Sam, and she and Matt got back in the car and headed for the parking spot. "Wow," Matt said. "That was as friendly a greeting as I've ever had at a golf course."

"It sure was."

Matt said, "No kidding! I noticed that there was something different when I called for a tee time. The guy I talked to in the pro shop was extremely helpful and gave perfect directions to the course."

"Really?"

"It made me wonder what kind of reception our prospects get when they first contact us. I'm not sure that our receptionist is as friendly as she needs to be, or that she could give anyone directions to our office," Matt remarked as he parked the car. "It will be interesting to see how other folks here treat us."

A friendly voice greeted them as they approached the registration counter. "Hi, I'm Dan Bennett, head pro of the course. You must be the Jennings twosome. Welcome!" Dan extended his hand to both Matt and Elizabeth.

Matt and Elizabeth looked at each other in amazement. The great customer-service experience they'd seen at the bag drop had followed them into the pro shop.

"You still have a few minutes before your tee time. Would you like some golf balls for the driving range?"

"That would be great," Matt responded. "We've got to get loosened up."

As Dan handed Matt and Elizabeth each a bag of balls, he said, "Make sure you come back to our pro shop after your round. We've got some great new golf clothes. And the latest driver from Callaway just came in—everybody loves it!"

"Thanks!" Elizabeth said, pushing the pro shop door open as she and Matt headed to the practice range.

"It's pretty hot out there, Mr. Jennings. Do you have a hat?" asked the young pro across the shop.

"You're right," Matt said. "I do need a hat."

Matt bought a hat, a ball marker with the course logo, a sleeve of balls, and a yardage book.

As they hit practice shots on the range, Matt and Elizabeth continued the conversation about the service they had already experienced that day.

"Matt," Elizabeth remarked after hitting a long straight practice drive, "if there is any one thing that I can really point to for my success, it's that my team really takes care of our customers. Too many organizations act like it would be easier if they didn't have to deal with their customers at all. They don't realize that it's their customers who bring them their paychecks."

Before taking his practice swing, Matt responded. "I wish everyone in my organization had that attitude."

"Look, we're not perfect, and we do make mistakes with our customers. When we do, though, we try to recover quickly. If your people don't already put your customers first, it's time you do something about it," said Elizabeth. "When you called me, you talked about the challenges that you've had in your company lately. The fastest way to get things turned around is to refocus on your customers."

"I hear what you're saying. Like I said before, unlike your prospects, I'm not sure that my prospective customers get as warm a greeting as they should when they first contact our company. But it goes beyond that. Experiencing the service we've gotten here so far today made me feel like *everyone* here deserves a tip. I've been to your business several times, and your team always seems to be so friendly. I bet they really are responsive to your customer's needs. How do you make that happen?"

"It boils down to the very basics. First of all, we hire the right people. We put everyone through a rigorous interview process and then spend the time and the money to invest in their future. Matt, you've got to be willing to invest in your team, make sure you hire the right people, and give them constant training."

Getting back into the golf cart, Matt expressed his frustration. "I'm drowning, Elizabeth. I don't have the time or the money for training right now!"

"You have to find the time—and the money! Training doesn't *cost*. It *pays*."

"I don't know, Elizabeth. You still have to have the money in order to do the kind of training you're talking about. When cash is tight, you have to weigh every expense. I need my folks out talking to and selling to our customers, not spending their time learning things they should already know."

"Hold that thought, Matt. Okay, now let's see how I'm hitting today," Elizabeth said as she put her clubs back in her bag.

Lessons from the Links

1. *Golfers play their games based on the condition of the course and their own skills—not on who they're paired with. Similarly, if business owners focused on their companies instead of their competitors, they'd be a lot more successful.*
2. *Golfers work to overcome their weaknesses and improve their strengths.*
3. *Business owners need to hire the right folks and invest in training them to deliver world-class customer service.*

First Hole:

Penciling in Your Score

"Joe shot his age twice today! Once on the front side and once on the back side."

First Hole:
Penciling in Your Score

As they got back into the cart to drive from the practice range to the first hole, Matt looked over and noticed that Elizabeth had taken the scorecard and penciled in a score for the round. As she put it back on the steering wheel, he looked at the score she'd written on the card. He remembered that she was a pretty good golfer, but the score on the card would be a stretch for her.

As they waited on the tee box, Matt's curiosity got the best of him. "Hey Elizabeth, what are you doing? How can you fill in your scorecard? We haven't even teed off yet!"

Having seen that kind of reaction before, Elizabeth was unfazed. "Don't worry; I won't cheat. I'll count every stroke, but that's what I hope to shoot today. I've been playing pretty well, but I'm always trying to get better. I've found that writing down what I'd like to shoot before every round has really helped my game. Once I've put it in writing, it's like a clear vision. It sets the bar for the day."

Matt still looked puzzled.

"Once I've decided what I want to shoot, I try to picture what I need to hit on each hole to get there. I know that I won't score as well on the longer holes as I will on the short par fours, so I have to develop a different strategy for each hole. If I beat my plan on a hole, great, I have some cushion. If I miss my goal on a hole, I've got my work cut out for me and I change my plan for another hole—not necessarily the next hole, because that one might not be the one on which I can most easily shave off a stroke."

"That makes sense."

"I do the same thing in my business. I opened my business because of this vision I had. I knew that it would take a long time and a lot of work to get there, but knowing where I am headed has made the long hours and the hard work easier. I can really feel what it's going to be like when I cross the imaginary finish line I've pictured all this time. I can taste that success."

"I get it," Matt said. "The score you decided you'll shoot today is like that finish line."

"Sort of. But like in my business, there's no guarantee that I'll get there easily. You know how unpredictable golf is, Matt; it's tricky."

"Yeah," he said, "the little pond on the ninth hole at my club is like a magnet for my ball. It doesn't matter what I do—I always seem to go right to it."

"That's the advantage of having a vision. It's sort of like using that yardage book you bought. You focus on the big picture and the end result instead of on the obstacles in the way. And if you dunk one and take a penalty, you know what you have to do to make it up and reach your goal for the round."

With a slight grimace Matt admitted, "That sounds a lot more sensible than throwing a club and having a small tantrum."

Elizabeth went on, "In my business, every day is different. We don't always have record-breaking sales each month, and an economic downturn hits us just like everyone else. Golf is the same way. Sometimes, the longest par five plays better than the easiest par three."

"It's harder to get a hole-in-one on a par five, though."

Elizabeth laughed and said, "You're right, but the point is that I don't worry about any one shot or any one hole on the course. I focus on playing to get to my goal. Doing that keeps me from getting rattled or giving up. I also don't get caught up on how the others in my foursome are playing. I'm playing against myself to get to the score I've decided I can shoot for that day, and I keep focused on that end.

"I run my business the same way. I've got a lot of competitors, and it seems like new ones keep popping up every day. Many of them are bigger than we are, and some of them seem to have an unlimited supply of capital."

"That's exactly what I'm facing right now. It feels as if there's someone new opening up every day."

After commenting that the flowers next to the cart path on the way to the first tee box were in full bloom, Elizabeth responded to Matt: "You can't spend your time worrying about your competitors' game plan. It would be like letting one bad shot or a double bogey ruin a whole round of golf. You've got to play your own game. You've got to keep concentrating on what you do well and trying to improve your skills."

She went on, "I've been studying how the tour pros play. I think the biggest difference between the best and the rest is consistency. The winners don't change their games based on who they're paired with. They play their own games all the time. They don't let up when they're ahead, and they don't quit when they're behind. I think they must envision wearing the green jackets or taking home the big money. And that makes *them* the competition—the ones to beat."

Matt took his driver and walked up to the tee box, nodding. He liked Elizabeth's outlook and the way she seemed to approach her business. It made a lot of sense. He was thinking about visions and goals and playing his own game.

He paused for a minute, staring down the fairway, and seemed almost in a trance as he looked toward the green. Matt put his ball on a tee and without even taking a practice swing hit a long, straight drive to the middle of the fairway. His drive left him with a short easy second shot to get to the green.

"Great drive," Elizabeth said as she walked to her tee box. "I thought you said you hadn't had time to play lately."

"That's true, but I think I've just remembered something important about this game. Instead of just bashing the ball, I created a picture of where I wanted it to go. Somehow, the ball got the message and landed right where I'd hoped it would."

Elizabeth smiled. "I don't think the ball got the message, Matt. I think you did."

Elizabeth's drive, although not quite as far as Matt's, was also solidly in the fairway.

Lessons from the Links

When she got back into the cart, she saw that Matt had turned the scorecard over and entered his hoped-for ending score right under hers.

First Hole: Penciling in Your Score

1. *Vision defines your finish line. You can't get there if you don't know where you're going. Develop a personal and a business vision.*
2. *Vision helps set short-term goals. Set goals and objectives to help you move toward your vision.*
3. *Put it in writing. The difference between a dream and a vision is the ability to clearly articulate your end games.*

Second Hole:

Playing from the Right Tee Box

"I found the ball but I lost my golf clubs!"

Second Hole:
Playing from the Right Tee Box

As Matt reached for his driver at the next hole, Elizabeth said, "I'm glad to see that you're playing from the front tees today, Matt. Last week I played with a couple who'd just started playing. The guy walked to the back tees every time he hit off. At first I thought he didn't know that he could go up to the front tees, so I told him the difference."

"Did he get it?" Matt asked.

"No, he just shrugged and said, 'Well, I'll have to play from back here sometime, so I might as well start now.' It took him forever to get to the green."

Matt parked the cart next to the tee box. "Well, I've played so little lately I know I'd never get to the green from the back tees."

"You're better than most, Matt."

"Some golfers don't understand that the different tees are to help make you successful at the game—you should always try to play to par, and your handicap determines which tees give you the best chance at getting there," Matt said.

"Yeah, I guess it's ego. If you think you're a better golfer than you really are, you'll want to hit from the longer tees, but in reality that gets in the way of getting to the green in regulation," said Elizabeth.

Matt nodded and said, "You know, ego can be great and it can be the worst part of us. Our egos make us try new things that would be daunting if we always thought we weren't good enough to do them. On the other hand, overly inflated egos have caused lots of people to fall. And when they hit bottom, they hit hard."

"There's a big difference between ego and self-confidence. You need them both, but you need to understand how they work together. Our best sales associates are plenty confident. They take time to get to know their customers, and they match our products to their customers' needs. They can get pretty competitive when a big deal is on the line. But for the most part, knowing their weaknesses helps them keep their egos in check. I think ego can be an appropriate expression of your self-esteem, but it can just as easily become an inflated opinion of yourself." Elizabeth explained.

"I know exactly what you mean. In business, you see big egos all the time. I have one client we always call Mr. Big. Every time one of my folks calls on him, Mr. Big goes on and on about his big deals and the great vacations he's going to take and the terrific things he's doing in the community. It's all about him," Matt said. "But the true picture of Mr. Big comes out every month when he's late in paying us. He complains about his cash flow and tries to get extended terms."

"Yeah, as business owners, it's easy to believe that you're more important than you really are. We have to keep it in perspective—our jobs, businesses, and careers are what we *do*, not who we *are*," Elizabeth said.

"It's good to have confidence—we have to believe in ourselves. Without some degree of self-confidence I think we'd all just stay in bed. And it's important to celebrate our victories. At the same time though, we have to make sure that we're not overly confident." Looking a bit sheepish, Matt went on, "I guess that's why it took me so long to see that I needed help and to reach out to you. We invest so much of ourselves into our businesses it almost defines us. It's no sin to ask for help—in fact, I'm starting to think it's kind of courageous."

Matt winced as his drive went straight for the bunker on the right.

"So okay, Matt. I know your ego's in check, but do you have the confidence to get out of this sand trap and onto the green?"

Unable to find a rake near the trap, Matt stepped in as gingerly as he could. "Sure; it's a piece of cake. Well, maybe not that easy, but I'm going to give it a try." Matt smiled and walked into the bunker.

Second Hole: *Playing from the Right Tee Box*

1. *Don't be afraid to play from the forward tees. Admitting your weaknesses helps overcome them.*
2. *Ego and confidence are both important human drivers. Beware of over-confidence and over-inflated egos.*
3. *Our careers are what we do ... not who we are.*
4. *Asking for help is courageous. Seek out a mentor, a trade association, a buying group, a consultant, or a business associate.*

Third Hole:

Communicating to Avoid Hazards

Third Hole:
Communicating to Avoid Hazards

As Matt got back into the cart after hitting his drive he asked, "So, Elizabeth what else makes your business tick?"

"Hmmm ..." She thought for a minute. "It took me a while to realize its importance, but communication is one of the real strengths in my organization."

"You mean the way you talk to each other?"

"No, the way we listen to each other."

"Listen?"

"Yes. Even in golf—one of the most individual sports around—you can learn a lot by watching how the pros interact with their caddies. Good pros really listen to what their caddies have to say."

"Sure, I've seen caddies suggest a club to their player, Elizabeth, but in the end it's the pro who makes the ultimate choice."

"Yes, but they use all the help they can get. A caddy is more than a person who carries a player's bag. They usually give insightful advice and moral support. A caddy is aware of the challenges and obstacles of the golf course being played, along with the best strategy in playing it. They'll know the overall yardage, where the hazards are, pin placements, and club selection."

"Hmmm. I've never played with a caddie, but I can sure see how they can help play a better game."

"I don't know about that, but your business might be better if you used your 'caddies' more effectively. I'm sure you've got folks on your team with years of experience. I bet if you'd give them a chance, they'd be happy to help you turn your business around."

"I've been afraid to tell them too much. I don't want them to think that we're going under. I don't want them talking to our suppliers or our customers about our problems."

"Don't kid yourself. They know exactly what's going on."

Elizabeth went on. "Joey Sindelar's caddy, John Buchna, has been with him a record-setting twenty-three years. I know Sindelar's had a lot of ups and downs on his way to winning seven PGA Tour events and over $11 million. Sindelar has said that his relationship with Buchna has lasted this long not only because John pulls the right club for him or because he reads greens so well but because they read each other's emotions really well. If it were just about carrying clubs, they'd start using carts on the tour."

"Okay. So, do I need more meetings?"

"There are hundreds of ways to get your message to your staff and for them to get their input to you. You need to use all the weapons in your arsenal.

"Sometimes I meet one on one with my staff, and other times I blast a message through our company intranet. There are also times when we hold group meetings—like the weekly meetings my sales team has. Every meeting has an agenda. Since it goes out a few days in advance, participants can add things to it. They're also prepared when they get to the meeting."

Matt shook his head, "We used to have a regular meeting schedule and everyone participated, but after a while our meetings got to be so stale that I finally quit having them. It seems like we kept rehashing the same issues every week. If I think about it, I guess they were more of a monologue than a real conversation. I told them what I thought they needed to know, and they nodded."

"That's why most meetings are so unproductive, Matt. You have to have a concrete reason to hold one—an expected outcome. If you just want to hand down information, put it in a memo and save everyone time."

"Maybe that's what we should do. People hate spending time in meetings."

"Only if they really *are* a waste, Matt. If people don't feel like they have any role in the meeting except for being spectators."

"I probably could do a better job of making my associates feel more comfortable about sharing their ideas with me, but I don't want to get too close to my people. Some of their ideas just aren't realistic. If I keep my distance I can keep my perspective."

"You don't have to act on everything your team suggests, but you have to actively listen to them. Make them feel safe in coming to you, and go out and ask their input whenever you can. If you really want to show them you're listening, carry a notebook and write down what you hear them telling you. They'll feel important, and you'll do a better job of hearing what's being said."

"There are other tools I have to communicate with my team members. I should probably update things like our policy and procedure manual and our job descriptions too," Matt said.

"Sure, Matt. The best way to get buy-in from your team is to have them create the updates. Let them review their own job descriptions and add or delete things as needed. If you have them help update the associate handbook, they'll remember things about the company they haven't thought of for a while."

"But I don't just want to rely on memos and manuals, Elizabeth. It sounds like you're pretty close to your associates."

"I am, because I value them and respect their contributions to the company. I can't run my business alone. I want my people to be a significant part of everything we do."

Matt responded, "I value my people when they're doing their jobs and when things are going well. When we're meeting our targets, I know they've done what they're supposed to. But at times like this …"

"No one wins all the time, Matt. When times are tough, that's when you all really need to pull together."

"Like a caddy is to a pro, huh?"

Elizabeth smiled as she teed up her ball.

Third Hole: Communicating to Avoid Hazards

1. *Listening is the most important part of good communication.*
2. *Actively listen and take notes.*
3. *Your staff members are your caddies—they are critical to playing a better game. You need their feedback to accomplish your objectives.*
4. *Make meetings productive with goals, agendas, and time limits.*
5. *Policy manuals and written procedures keep everyone on the same page.*

Fourth Hole:

Playing with the Right Team

**"If you don't believe an eight,
would you believe a seven?"**

Fourth Hole:
Playing with the Right Team

As they drove down the cart path to the fourth hole, Matt noticed three groundskeepers moving a heavy pipe. "We've seen some examples of great teamwork at this golf course," Matt said.

"Sure have!"

"It's pretty unusual."

"At least on a golf course."

"Everyone we've met here has a great attitude. They've talked about their other team members as if they were family—and friends!" Elizabeth noted.

"Starting with Sam at the bag drop, who called in our names to the pro shop so that they knew who we were when we walked in."

"It's terrific." Matt stopped as the course ranger drove up to them.

"It's a matter of hiring the right people and building a culture of trust."

"Come on," Matt chimed in. "My team can't get past the rumors, gossip, and finger pointing, much less have trust in each other."

"Doesn't sound much like a team to me!"

"Is your staff a team?" Matt asked.

"Nobody's perfect, but they work extremely well together," Elizabeth answered. "I'm very proud of our teamwork."

"Come on ..."

"It's true. Teamwork is a vital part of every successful organization, including mine."

"How do you do it?"

"As I mentioned, Matt, trust is a key ingredient. But it takes more than just trust. Our team has several other skills that help them to work together. They have common goals. Our team members helped write our strategic plan, and they are actively involved in updating that plan every quarter."

"Every quarter?"

"Yes. With today's economic uncertainty we're constantly reviewing our plan."

"Where do you find the time?"

"Actually, Matt, planning saves us time. By having common goals, we're not spending all of our time fighting each other and working in a million different directions. The planning process pays for itself a thousand times over."

"Okay," said Matt, "you've built your team with trust and in having common goals. What else?"

"Our team members are accountable, and they don't play the 'blame game.' There's a fine line between blame and accountability. There's no room for blame in our company—or in yours. That's where the stories, gossip, and finger pointing come from.

"Matt, I'm sure that Michelle, Chris, Sam, and others we've met here today all work for tips, but they realize that the customer's satisfaction is the most important thing. They work together as a team to make that happen."

"It's pretty impressive."

"It's one of the reasons why it's so difficult to get a tee time here."

"You're right about that."

"They must have common goals. And it's obvious that they trust each other and don't spread blame around."

"I'll bet they all take ownership as well," Elizabeth remarked. "And with that comes accountability."

By this time, they were approaching the fourth green.

"I'm on in two," Matt proudly stated. "I hit a fantastic drive, and my seven iron has me set to make a birdie. Now if I can just get my putter to be a good team player!"

Elizabeth laughed as they headed toward the green, reflecting on their conversation, hoping that Matt got the message about the need for a stronger team.

Fourth Hole: Playing with the Right Team

1. *Teamwork is vital to success. Create high-functioning teams by ensuring that all members understand the importance of each person's role and that each member respects his or her coworkers.*

2. *Trust is key in team building. A sales associate, for instance, has to have confidence that others on his team give his customers the same kind of attention that he would—and he has to trust that someone filling in for him won't steal either the customer or his commission.*

3. *Teams share common goals. Just like winning the Super Bowl or the Stanley Cup, business teams must pull together towards predetermined targets. The team gains strength from the way each member fits into the whole.*

4. *Accountability, not blame, creates healthy teams. Each team member serves a vital role and has a responsibility to do his or her part to ensure that the team is successful. Even the receptionist plays a vital role. If the telephone isn't answered quickly, the company could lose a new customer, causing everyone to miss the month's sales quota.*

Fifth Hole:

Even Golf Is about the Brand

"I'm sure we'll hear about his hole-in-one!"

Fifth Hole:
Even Golf Is about the Brand

As they drove to the fifth hole, Matt said, "Compared to most golfers, I'm not very brand loyal. Unless I get them for gifts I don't wear Tommy Bahama shirts like the guy we saw on the driving range. I don't really have a favorite golf ball. But I sure seem to play better with my Calloway Big Bertha than with any other driver I've owned. I had a couple of other oversized clubs before, and they were okay, but a few years ago I rented a set of clubs on a business trip and they came with a Big Bertha and I got hooked."

Elizabeth said, "That's the big mystery of branding, Matt. Sometimes a name brand really does perform better than its competitors, and other times it's just fashion or media hype. There's a lot to be said for the power of the brand. You know, maybe one of the problems in your business is your branding."

"My branding?"

"Yeah," Elizabeth said, "your branding."

Matt furrowed his brow, "We're not in a fashion business. The products and services we sell aren't rare, trendy, or glitzy. They're more run-of-the mill than glamorous. "

Elizabeth asked, "Are they different from your competitors' products?"

"Yeah."

"Are they better?"

"Sure."

Lessons from the Links

"Your brand has to help you describe those differences. When people think of your company, your brand will help them instantly recognize the quality of the products and services you offer. Your brand should create your customers' expectations."

Matt looked toward Elizabeth. "I understand how branding differentiates places like McDonalds from Ruth's Chris Steak House. In the restaurant business your brand has to promise something to bring customers to your place. But I'm still not sure ..."

"Okay, Matt, let's take golf courses. Which ones do you think are the *best* in the world?"

"That's easy—Pebble Beach, St. Andrews, the Ocean Course at Kiawah Island, Pinehurst, Medinah, Oakland Hills. And certainly Augusta!"

"Have you played those courses?" Elizabeth asked.

"Not all of them," Matt admitted.

"Then how do you know they're the best?"

Matt suddenly visualized himself playing on one of these famed golf courses. "Well, I guess it's their reputation. They draw the biggest tournaments. They're exclusive—you can't even play Augusta unless you're one of their few members. They have signature holes, and they're designed by the best pros."

Elizabeth went on, "How about the *prettiest* golf courses?"

"There are bunch of beautiful clubs in Hawaii. Certainly, the floating hole at the Coeur d'Alene in Idaho is one of the most spectacular."

"You played that one?"

"No."

"That's the power of branding, Matt. Their brands peg Augusta and Pinehurst as exclusive. And without having been to Idaho, you can picture playing the floating fourteenth hole at the Coeur d'Alene. Because of its brand you have a mental image—a picture of the experience you'd get there—of what you'd find on a given golf course even though you may not have ever played there. In golf courses, the brand is extended every time a big tournament is televised. You can't watch the Masters without noticing the beautiful dogwoods and azaleas around the course."

"I get you," Matt said. "And there are different golf courses for different people. If you're a beginner, you might be more comfortable playing at a municipal course than at a fancy country club. Even more than saving some money, you might feel more at home at a city course with folks who play more like you do."

"Right. And some courses won't let you walk, while others will only let you drive their golf carts on the cart paths—not on the fairways. If you want to find the best caddies, Scottish courses like St. Andrews would be the place to go."

Matt nodded in agreement. "Some golf courses are branded by their pros or by their golf schools. Some clubs differentiate themselves by their youth programs or by their ability to plan really special charity golf tournaments. Some courses are just great places for family fun.

"It might work. Maybe if I develop a better brand, my customers will know exactly what they'll get in doing business with us. They'll know what to expect from *our* people, *our* products, and *our* services.

"At the same time we can use our brand to differentiate ourselves from others in the business. If we have a strong brand, people will know that the only place they can get our products delivered by our team members with our kind of after-sale service is from us."

"Bingo! I think you're catching on. Now let's see if you can put your drive on the fairway!"

Fifth Hole: Even Golf Is about the Brand

1. Branding is one of the most powerful marketing tools you can develop. Your brand builds a mental picture for your customers, vendors, community, and team members. It's a promise of what one will get when doing business with you.
2. Just like McDonald's is different from Ruth's Chris Steak House, your brand helps target your audience and establish your product and service assortment.
3. Rookie golfers might feel more comfortable at city courses, while low handicappers might prefer exclusive private clubs. Hikers and campers might opt for a Subaru, while a red BMW convertible is right for other drivers. Branding has significant influence on the buying decisions we make.
4. Knowing about your target customer, the traits that differentiate your business from others, and the benefits of the products and services you offer will help you articulate your brand.

Sixth Hole:

Even the Best Clubs Don't Sell Themselves

"I sold everything! I even got ten dollars for those silly golf clubs of yours!"

Sixth Hole:
Even the Best Clubs Don't Sell Themselves

As they approached the sixth green surrounded by deep sand traps that they'd both managed to avoid, Matt asked, "Elizabeth, your company has great products, and your organization seems to make sales a lot easier than mine does. What kind of secret sauce do your salespeople have?"

After a moment's reflection, Elizabeth asked, "Do you remember the young pro in the pro shop today? When you approached the counter, he noticed that you weren't wearing a hat and asked if you'd like to buy one. When you said you would, he didn't just point you in the direction of the hats; he took you over to them. He showed you several different designs and seemed genuinely interested in helping you find one you really liked. And when you got back to the desk, he suggested that you buy a yardage book for the course, since this is the first time you have played it."

"Yes, I felt that he was helpful, not pushy. I appreciated his help."

"Now relate that to a few months ago when we played at the golf club on the north side of town. As I remember, you wanted to look at a new putter, but the guy behind the counter just pointed to their display. He was anything but helpful. He didn't respond to your buying signal, even though you gave every indication that you were ready to spend big bucks on a new putter."

Lessons from the Links

"Gee, I guess you're right, Elizabeth. I really was ready to buy a putter but needed some help to decide which one to buy. They had a great selection, but since no one helped me I ended up waiting until later in the week, when I went to one of those discount golf shops. But today, the pro made me aware of the needs I had and then made it easy to fill those needs. But what does that have to do with the difference in the selling success of your company—and the struggles that I'm having?"

"Matt, although we're in different kinds of businesses selling different products, we have the same challenges when it comes to sales. The difference is that my team understands that things have changed. Years ago, you and I could just about wait for the phone to ring and then fill the orders as customers came in or called us. Today, *your* sales team is still just taking orders. *My* sales team is helping our customers solve their specific problems. They ask a lot of questions to see what our prospects need. There's a big difference."

"You're right, Elizabeth. The phones just aren't ringing the way they did a few years ago, and my market share has dropped a lot. But there's not much I can do to make customers want or need to buy my stuff."

"We've noticed changes in our customers' behavior as well. The phone may not ring as often, but we're getting more and more traffic on our Web site every month. What percentage of your sales comes from your Web site, Matt?"

"Oh, we don't sell our products on our Web site. It just has information about our company and our products. We only have it to keep up with the competition. You know, it's for our image."

"Matt, 20 percent of our sales come from our Web site, compared to just 5 percent three years ago."

"But doesn't that cause problems with your direct sales force? Don't they complain that they lose sales to the Internet?"

"Not at all," Elizabeth replied. "Part of my company's vision is to work together to gain as much market share as possible. Our Web site helps the direct sales team, and the direct sales team helps drive sales to our Web site. New customer inquiries are funneled to our sales force for follow-up. The associate can be sure the buyer knows about the other services and products we offer. We make sure we have a multidimensional relationship with our online customers. We want them to know that if they need sales assistance, we have professionals on staff to take care of them."

"But I also sell some of my products at retail," Matt argued. "If we sold those products on the Internet we'd end up closing down all our stores."

"Matt, I talked to a friend who visited Best Buy's corporate headquarters in Minneapolis. All over the main floor, there were signs that said, "www.BestBuy.com—Our biggest store!" They understand the potential of the Internet, and constantly reinforce the idea that their retail stores must work hand in hand with their Web site. It's not an 'us versus them' mentality. It's all about their customers. You can now research and make your purchase on their Web site and pick it up at the store nearest you.

"Your Web site and sales force have to work together, Matt. They should create synergies for each other and make it easier for your customers to buy your products. They won't compete but will help you build your brand, improve your market share, and create top-of-the-mind awareness. It doesn't matter where your business comes from, just as long as it grows."

Matt still didn't seem he convinced. He shook his head as he stepped up to line up his putt. He looked even more mystified when his putt sailed six feet past the hole. He missed his next putt too, settling for a double-bogey on the hole.

As they got back in the cart, Matt said, "So, I have to go from taking orders to solving problems for my customers. And I have to figure out how to sell my products on the Internet. I can hire someone to work on my Web site, but how do I get my salespeople to make the transition from order takers to sales consultants?"

Elizabeth looked back to make sure they weren't holding up the group behind them, and said, ""We may have to talk about that some other time, Matt."

Sixth Hole: Even the Best Clubs Don't Sell Themselves

1. Selling is an art and takes great skill. Unless you run a fast-food store, you probably can't afford to have "order takers" on your team. Trained sales professionals add value to your business.
2. Today's customer demands multiple purchase options. Some buy on the telephone; some from a sales associate; and others prefer to buy online. A good Web site will generate new customers, buyer inquiries, and increased sales.
3. Web sales do not compete with other selling platforms. In many cases they are made to new customers and add new revenues. It's all about giving customers what they want, when they want it and how they want it.

Seventh Hole:

Dealing with Hazards

"I don't think Charlie is ever going to get out of that trap!"

Seventh Hole:
Dealing with Hazards

"I can't believe how much water there is on this course," Matt complained. His approach shot to the seventh green had just missed the creek behind the green.

"Did you see the guy in the group ahead of us hit his shot right into the water? At least you're safe this time. Most golf courses have hazards, Matt. And so does every business."

"You're right. My competition is driving me nuts, the morale in my organization is at an all-time low, and just when things seem like they can't get much worse, there's some pending legislation that could cost me thousands of dollars a year."

"Matt, just as you have to figure out how to keep your ball out of the drink, you also have to find ways to deal with the hazards in your business. Of course, the best strategy in both golf and business is to stay out of the hazards, but even the best golfers get in trouble at times. With business, we need to avoid as many of the traps as we can, but we need to deal with these challenges as they hit us."

"You haven't hit into the water all day. It's only the seventh hole and I've already been in it twice. I also drove the ball into the sand trap on the third hole."

"Maybe part of your problem is that you usually go for the risky shot. On this hole, I chose to play my second shot short of the green to leave an easy approach shot. You tried to hit a very long shot to a green that's surrounded with bunkers and the creek, and you nearly paid the price. The same thing happened when you hit the ball in the water."

"It's just not my nature to play conservative. I'm not a big risk taker in my business, but I make up for it out here."

"I'm not telling you to play it safe with every shot; however, you can't always go for the long shot. The same thing applies to your business. You have to take some risks. I think you told me that you bought some equipment lately that wasn't as good as it could have been. You were afraid to buy the entire system, and it's cost you because it's not doing the job that you need it to do. There's a relationship between risk and reward."

"Yes, I was trying to limit my risk and save money and took a chance that this stuff would work, and it's been a real nightmare."

"You're in a business hazard. You have to accept the fact that you bought the wrong equipment and figure out how to deal with it."

"But how about the competition? They keep cutting their prices, and I'm losing one account after another."

"You can't control the competition, but you can find ways to stay ahead of them. You seem to spend a lot of time complaining about them but not enough time looking for ways to win new customers."

"I wish there were fewer business hazards."

"Matt, hazards are part of life. It's reality. Instead of spending your time worrying about them, learn how to recognize when you're in one and what to do to get out of it. Your team will be much more productive when you change your mind-set."

"Well, it's certainly not going to help with penalty strokes I had to take when I landed in the drink."

Elizabeth smiled broadly, "No, it won't, Matt. But hopefully, you'll try harder to avoid the hazards. Besides, with the practice you've had, you're really getting the hang of that sand wedge and ball retriever."

Seventh Hole: Dealing with Hazards

1. *Try to avoid hazards.*
2. *When you get into one, know how to get out with the least penalty.*
3. *Understand the relationship between risk and reward.*

Eighth Hole:

You Can't Buy a Game

"Don't be too impressed. Ed got it at a garage sale."

Eighth Hole:
You Can't Buy A Game

While they waited on the eighth tee box for the group in front of them to clear the fairway, Matt walked past Elizabeth's bag and said, "Elizabeth, you're playing great golf today, and it looks like you've had those clubs for years. I always buy the latest and greatest clubs, and they don't seem to work any better than my old ones."

"I can't tell you how many times I've tried to 'buy a game,' Matt. For a long time, I'd read *Golf* magazine and see a review of some new club and run out and buy it without even trying it first. One time, I went to a guy who made custom clubs and spent a fortune on a new set. My game hit an all-time low, and it took me a couple of seasons before I admitted that they weren't right for me.

"From what you've told me, you do the same thing in your business. You're always buying new technology, from computers to sales-automation software. Don't you sometimes wonder whether it's worth your investment?"

"How else do you keep up?"

"The first step is to understand that spending money on new equipment and software won't solve all your problems. When it comes to technology, I give my team everything they need to accomplish our goals, but that doesn't mean we've always got the 'latest and greatest.' In fact, when we do invest in computers, software, and other gear, we don't just consider the dollars we spend, but also the learning process that is an investment in my team's time."

Lessons from the Links

"So, how do you decide when to buy a new computer—or a new golf club?"

"With golf, that's easy. The manufacturers would like us to buy a new set of irons every year. But let's face it, how much difference can it make from year to year? At times, there are breakthroughs, like when they started making 'woods' out of metal, when graphite shafts were introduced, and when Odyssey brought out their 'two-ball' putter. If I still used a wooden driver or three 'wood,' I'd be way behind the game. The same is true for any purchase I make in business. It's all about choices."

As the fairway finally cleared ahead of them, Matt hit his tee shot and then turned to Elizabeth. "You may be right. I'm not sure my company is actually more productive after most of the purchases we make. And we always seem to be spending a lot of time trying to learn how to use new equipment or how to make the transition from the old software to the new stuff. But I know that without up-to-date stuff, we'll fall behind. I think that could just make things even worse. I just don't always make the best choices."

"Matt, I was playing golf with a friend and she told me, 'I might be out-played, but I'll never be out-teched.' In other words, she would always buy the latest piece of golf equipment so that she never let her competitors have an equipment advantage over her. But there's a happy medium between buying all the latest technology and staying with the old equipment too long. Again, it's about choices. In addition, what works for you, in golf or in business, may not work best for me. If I try to hit your new driver, it may have the wrong loft or shaft for my game. And you're taller than me; I'd have to choke up on the club.

"In business, what works well for me may be too much for you, and vice versa. When you make any major investment, though, you have to do a cost-benefit analysis. What kind of return are you going to get? Is the new computer system going to make your sales team more productive? Is the new customer-relations management system going to bring you additional sales?"

"I guess I get too caught up in the pitch from all the salespeople, and even from my own team members who want me to buy new stuff."

"You have to be objective about your purchasing decisions. Your company is in a downturn right now, and spending money on new

You Can't Buy a Game

equipment is not always the best way to come out of that. At the same time, you can't be afraid to spend money on the things that you really need. Most companies cut back on things like advertising and training when their business slows up. However, cutting back on marketing will usually have an adverse effect on your sales. And training is the last thing I would ever cut back on."

Elizabeth hit her tee shot and then showed Matt her driver. "My driver is a good example. I bought it several years ago, when the manufacturers first came out with the oversized drivers. It helped my game. It was a definite change in technology. I hit several 'demo' models to determine which was best for me, and I chose this one. The year after I bought it, Titleist came out with an updated model. I tried it and found very little difference. Why buy something new just to have it? However, that was a few years ago, and I'm probably ready to buy a new driver. My driver is 'oversized,' but not like the drivers that we saw in the clubhouse.

"Another thing, Matt. I can have the same driver as Ernie Els, but that's probably not what's best for me. I have to buy what's best for my golf game—and for my business."

"We bought into a sales pitch that the software company's salesperson gave us. She made us think that this new software would revolutionize the way that we did our accounting. However, installing that software caused us fits. It does a lot of things that our old software couldn't do, and it is customized for my industry, but I'm not sure that the amount we spent and the long hours of adapting to the new software was worth our investment."

"In dollars and in training time, Matt. And I'll bet that the software company has tried to sell you on upgrades since the day you bought it."

"They sure are! In fact, we just bought the latest version."

"And?"

"Again, I'm not sure that the upgrade has been worth the time and money."

"And?"

"And I'd better learn how to be more objective in our buying decisions and to separate my personal involvement in wanting to always

♀ **57** ♀

have the latest and greatest from what we really need. How can I do that, Elizabeth?"

"It takes practice, Matt. Just like hitting your second shot on this hole. You have Cobra's newest irons to clear the water in front of the green, but will this five iron really do a better job than the five iron that you traded in to get these new clubs?"

With that, Elizabeth took out her "old" metal five wood and hit a beautiful shot to the green.

"You're tough competition, Elizabeth."

"Learn to make the better decisions, Matt, and your competition will say the same thing about you."

Eighth Hole: You Can't Buy a Game

1. *Be sure you get a solid return on investment when you purchase new equipment. Increased sales, productivity, or profits may warrant additional investment.*
2. *Newer isn't always better. Be objective when deciding if a new truck, computer, or software upgrade will really improve your business.*
3. *When business slows down, investment in advertising, marketing, and training may have a better payback than buying new technology or equipment.*

Ninth Hole:

Winners Never Stand Still

"A hole in one! This is my lucky day!"

Ninth Hole:
Winners Never Stand Still

"Not again!" Matt cried out as the wind caught his tee shot on the ninth hole. "That wind!"

"Don't blame the wind," Elizabeth responded.

"But my ball started out okay, and the wind took it right into the rough!"

"Matt, wind and rain are part of the game of golf. By now, you should be used to it. "

"I just don't like them."

"Or is it that you don't want to have to adapt to the conditions at hand?" Elizabeth asked.

"Now wait a minute; I know the world isn't stationary, but I don't like change on the golf course—just like I can't stand it when things change in my business."

"Aha, that's the challenge."

"What's that?"

"Your resistance to change. From what you say, Matt, I think you understand that business today is in a constant state of flux, but you seem unwilling to take action and change the way you do business.

"Sometimes I'm just not sure what direction to take and what changes will pay off. It seems easier just to do what we know rather than tumble into unknown waters. I guess I'm comfortable playing it safe."

"Matt, 'playing safe' may be the biggest risk you can take!"

"What do you mean?"

"Years ago, we could pretty well predict the future. That's just not true anymore. In my industry, there has been more change in the past five years than there was in the previous fifty! I'll bet yours is the same."

"Well, yes. I guess you could say that. But what do I have to do? I can't become a wild gambler and roll the dice every day."

"Wait a minute, Matt. Even when things are going well, you have to keep making changes to stay ahead of the game. Look at Tiger Woods!"

"What about Tiger?"

"If you remember, in his first Masters tournament as a professional, Tiger won by twelve strokes. But right after that, he completely changed his swing. Even though he blew the field away, he knew he needed to change. The same goes for your business."

"It's not easy. I was doing pretty well until my biggest competitor started importing some of their products. I wish things would just stay the same for a while. Just 'til I can right the ship."

"That's not reality. Before Tiger Woods turned thirty, he made two major revisions in his swing. It would have been easy for him to 'stay the course,' but he knew he had to make the changes to stay ahead of his competition. You need to do the same in your business. You need to constantly look for new ideas and put them into your game plan before your competition does."

Elizabeth went on. "First you have to get everyone on your team to stop fighting change—starting with yourself!"

"I didn't say I wouldn't change, just that I didn't like it. I knew I had to start doing things different—that's why I wanted to talk to you. I know that the world is shifting. I can't keep up with everything changing at once."

"Things aren't just changing, Matt—they're exploding! The biggest challenge about change now is the pace of the transformation. And I'll bet the pace of change in your industry is pretty fast now, too. Matt, you not only need to accept change—you and your team members have to embrace it!"

"Ugh!"

"Matt, even in good times, organizations need to constantly evolve. In fact, it's sometimes more difficult to see the 'Sand Trap of Success.'"

"What's that?" Matt asked.

"My third year in business, our company doubled in size. Things were going great—articles were being written about me, I was asked to speak at countless business events, and everything was about as good as it can get. Looking back, I started to get too comfortable with 'the status quo' and started to try and hold on to what I already had. I stopped taking calculated risks, and my business actually started to decline. Like the pros, I had to learn to keep changing even when things were going well. The status quo is what should cause your discomfort."

"With everything up in the air like it is now, it's kind of like the wind on the golf course. I don't know how to manage the business environment that I'm faced with now. It doesn't feel like a good time to make major changes."

"Matt, you need to maximize the 'opportunity of unrest' in your business. Get your team to be comfortable with these changing times and not to hold onto the status quo. When you play in the wind, you have to realize what it will do. When the wind is against you, use an extra club. When it's behind you, know that the ball isn't going to stop when it hits the green. Don't fight it—accept it, and use it to your advantage when the time is right."

"But I'm not a tour pro."

"That doesn't mean that you can't learn from them."

"Okay, Elizabeth. I'll use a five iron for this shot instead of the six iron that I normally hit from 160 yards."

"And use your natural swing, Matt."

With that, Matt hit a shot left of the green. He had enough distance but still had to work on his accuracy.

"One lesson at a time," Elizabeth thought to herself.

Ninth Hole: Winners Never Stand Still

1. *Change in business is like wind in golf—just part of the game.*
2. *Playing it safe may be the greatest risk. Failing to adapt to changing customer demographics or integrating new products into your mix may open the door for your competitors.*
3. *Beat your competition to the punch. Anticipate market changes and use them to your advantage. Be a leader, not a follower.*

Tenth Hole:

You've Gotta Play by the Rules

"Stroke and distance for out of bounds, play the ball as it lies . . . <u>this</u> can't be right!"

Tenth Hole:
You've Gotta Play by the Rules

After a brief stop in the clubhouse, Matt and Elizabeth got to the tenth hole just as the last man in the group ahead of them was teeing off. They quietly watched him take a practice swing and step up to address his ball. The breeze from his bad swing knocked the ball off of his tee and left it lying two inches in front of the tee. He looked around to see if anyone had seen him, quickly re-teed the ball, and hit his drive.

"I have a feeling he's not counting that as a stroke," Elizabeth said.

"I think you're right. Golfers who don't play by the rules tend to lack integrity in other areas of their lives. I see it all the time. I have a neighbor who says that just paying for a ball that gets lost in the woods or in the water is penalty enough. He rarely adds a penalty stroke, and he won't hesitate to take a mulligan every time he hits a bad drive. He also constantly parks in the fire lane in our alley. I know he gives his clients a discount for paying him in cash, and I suspect he doesn't report that money as income. I don't play with him much anymore because it's just not right."

"I know what you mean. I've seen people move their balls to get a better lie without even thinking about it. One of the good things about this game is that we're all responsible for our own scoring. We have the opportunity to test our own ethics in every round."

"I remember the first time I got a brochure for a class on business ethics. I couldn't figure out why anyone would need it. It's stuff we learned as kids—the Golden Rule and all of that," Matt said. "And now I hear all this news about real breaches in corporate America and I guess it's not so elementary."

"It's not always easy to do the right thing, Matt. One of my suppliers recently offered me a kickback if I'd agree to promote his products instead of his competitors'," Elizabeth said. "Instead of his getting more business from me, I bought less. I just didn't think he had the kind of integrity that I value in a relationship. I'm sure he went right down the street and offered the same kind of thing on his next sales call."

"I know what you mean. One of my biggest rivals continually promises his customers more than he can really deliver. Many of my new customers are people who haven't gotten what he'd said they would," Matt said. "And I know another guy who has bragged to me about how he's reduced his payroll by paying his laborers under the table. He's not only cheating the government; he's not really being fair to his team either.

"Things don't seem as black and white as they used to be. I mean, in golf, the USGA has a rule book that tells us what to do in just about every situation. You know what to do if you think your ball is out of bounds or if you hit into some kind of man-made hazard. You know when you have to take a penalty stroke and when you get a free drop.

"But in business, we're always negotiating, and sometimes that means you don't quite tell the whole story. I may tell a supplier I can get a better price somewhere else when I've never really priced his competitor. That's just kinda the way things are."

"You're right, Matt. In an effort to steal business from me I know that some of my competitors outright lie about the kind of service they think I can deliver. I can't spend all of my time defending myself. I just have to try to do my best to rise above the fray."

"Sometimes things that may be legal might still not be the right thing to do," Matt said.

"Look, no one's perfect. It's really hard to keep up with every change in the tax law or with every OSHA regulation or to be as 'green' as I'd like, but I really do believe that what my mother said still holds true."

"What's that?" Matt asked.

"You can never go wrong being right," she said. "Now go ahead and hit. And don't forget—I'm watching you."

Tenth Hole: You've Gotta Play by the Rules

1. *Just like the rules determined by the USGA for golf, business is ruled by ethics—by doing the right thing for your customers, suppliers, and team members.*
2. *Under-the-table payments, fraudulent tax reporting, and negotiating dishonestly can cost businesses clients, profits, and reputation.*
3. *Honesty is the best policy. It's better to tell a customer that you'll be late on a delivery or that you misquoted a price than to try to explain the problem as a misunderstanding or a failure to communicate.*

Eleventh Hole:

Finding the Time to Play

"I can't talk to you right now, honey, I'm in the middle of an important business meeting."

Eleventh Hole:
Finding the Time to Play

Elizabeth's tee shot when straight down the fairway, landing just in front of the green. "Great shot, Elizabeth. You're sure playing a great game today. You must play all the time."

"Well, not all the time, Matt. I've got a couple of other hobbies that keep me busy, and my kids still take a lot of my time."

"I've had to lay off a couple of people, and now I spend so much time at work I barely have time for anything else."

"Yeah, I guess that's pretty common today. Everyone seems to be wearing lots of hats, and it's hard to keep all the balls in the air. I've learned that time can get away from you if you're not careful."

"So, what kind of things do you do so that you have time for everything?"

"Well, it may sound basic, Matt, but every day I make a to-do list. It feels great when I cross things off. When I update my list again the following morning, sometimes I'll just choose not to bring unfinished tasks forward because I realize they're not really important."

"Hmmm."

"And I prioritize my task list so that I do the most important things first. I try to tackle big projects and things that will have the greatest impact early in the day when I have the most energy."

"That makes sense, Elizabeth, but sometimes things like answering telephone calls or solving customer problems can throw my whole day off track. And e-mail …"

"As good as the Internet is it can be a real time bandit. I used to spend the whole day just checking my e-mail. Now I program myself to go into my e-mail every few hours and no more. It's a tough discipline, but I'm sure more productive now."

"I feel that I'm disciplined; it's just that there's too much to do and not enough time."

"Unless you can figure out how to extend the day, Matt, you'll have to work smarter to fit it all in."

"Maybe I could do a better job with all the telephone calls I get. If I just shut the phone off for a few hours every morning I could get a lot more done."

"You sure would. I've also had to create a new strategy for getting to bigger projects like strategic planning and marketing.

"It's tough enough to keep on top of all the day-to-day stuff, let alone find time for those things."

"Matt, if I waited until I could carve out five or six hours to play eighteen holes I wouldn't get out very often. Sometimes, I can only get out to play nine, so I just do that. Other times, I only have time to go out and hit a bucket of balls—like between my kids' games or something like that. And sometimes, I can only find fifteen or twenty minutes to practice my putting or hit a few chips, so I just do that."

"I think I see how you'd apply that to your business, Elizabeth. I bet you take big projects and break them down into manageable pieces that you can do in a short time."

"Right. Instead of waiting until I have three or four days to tackle something like budgeting, I'll put aside a morning to do the revenue budget for one department and meet with my controller about the expenses later that week. Because my team members are just as busy, we schedule a series of meetings over a couple of weeks each quarter to review our strategic plan."

"It doesn't feel like the way I'm used to doing things. I like moving from one thing to another all day. I've never been one for loads of planning. Still, I suspect I could get a lot more done just by developing a plan for spending my time while I'm at work. I'd feel like I accomplished more, too. And I probably really would have time for myself," Matt said as he walked to his ball.

"Exactly!"

Eleventh Hole: Finding the Time to Play

1. *Create a to-do list every day. It feels great to cross off the things you've completed. Prioritize the list—tackle the most important items or the most difficult ones in the morning while you're fresh.*

2. *Develop a plan for checking e-mail and answering telephone calls at special times in the day so that you can focus on more important things.*

3. *Break large projects like strategic planning and budgeting into several smaller tasks; put time lines on completing each of them so that the entire project is completed in a timely manner.*

Twelfth Hole:

You've Gotta Keep Score

"Age, nothing - I'd be satisfied to play my weight."

Twelfth Hole:
You've Gotta Keep Score

As they waited for the group in front of them to hit, Matt totaled their scores for the front nine and said, "Now here's a number I can be happy with."

"You know, there's another way that golf is like business," said Elizabeth as they drove toward the next tee box.

"Yeah, what's that?"

"Keeping score."

"How do you mean?"

"Well, when I first started playing golf, I didn't worry much about my score. I was just trying to hit my ball a hundred yards and keep it out of the rough. I'd pick up my ball after two or three putts 'cause I didn't want to hold up my group.

"Every once in a while, I'd try to keep score, but I was taking eight or ten strokes a hole, so I figured why bother. But as I got more serious about the game, I decided to try counting my strokes. First I just counted putts—I only tried to keep from three-putting too often. I started to get better and made myself putt in each time I took three. I got pretty compulsive and started tracking my putting average 'til I actually got just over two."

Matt smiled, and Elizabeth went on.

"Once I saw that working, I decided I'd better start counting all my strokes. It was pretty scary for a while—I had some tough rounds—but keeping score and counting *all* my strokes made me spend more time on the driving range. I even took lessons every week for a whole summer."

"I get it. You started to play better once you knew how well you really were shooting."

"Yep. Then I started tracking my handicap and … well, you know how that is. There's never a low enough handicap."

"I see the parallel. The score I keep in my business is the bottom line. And that's why I'm so frustrated right now," said Matt.

"What else do you track?"

"I keep a pretty good eye on my inventory levels and my payroll."

"How about sales productivity? Do you know which of your associates delivers the highest gross margin or who adds the most additional items to each sale?"

"No."

"We measure our associates based on their margin, their total sales, their average sale, and the number of individual items on each transaction. From time to time—like during promotions or contests—we track other things as well. Without measuring their productivity, I can't coach my team and they can't help us meet our goals."

"That makes sense," said Matt.

"Do you ever run out of cash, Matt?"

"Doesn't everybody?"

"I never took an accounting class, and I hated math in school. When I started my business, I just figured that if I had good products and sold enough of them, it would work out. That was fine until the first time I couldn't meet my payroll or pay my suppliers."

"What did you do?"

"In the short run, Matt, I had to borrow some money from my family. Ultimately, though, I learned to manage my balance sheet."

"I hardly look at that, but my accountant says that if I did, I'd have a better handle on my business."

"And you'd know as much about your business as your bankers do, because they are really more interested in balance sheets than income statements."

"Why's that?" Matt asked. "I rely on my accountant to tell me what's going on. I assume that if there's a problem, he'll let me know."

"Your balance sheet tells you what you *own*—your assets—and what you *owe*—your liabilities. It's your report card and shows how much debt you carry and how much equity you have in your business.

"The more you understand about your balance sheet, the more quickly you'll be able to make changes that can significantly impact your performance. You could reduce inventory or start collecting your receivables more quickly to avoid getting into a cash crunch."

"I guess the income statement I study doesn't do quite the same thing, huh, Elizabeth?"

"You need them both. You need to spend some time every month analyzing them for trends so that you can make changes quickly. If you see sales declining on your income statement, you obviously need to cut your expenses. But it's probably also a signal to postpone buying new fixed assets or extending terms on your accounts payable so that you can increase your cash position."

"So, I need to track my sales productivity, keep an eye on sales and expenses, and learn to manage my balance sheet, right?"

"Well, you should also develop a cash flow statement, and ..."

Shaking his head, Matt suddenly looked overwhelmed. "Maybe what you're really saying is that I've grown past my ability to run by the seat of my pants. It seems like business has gotten more complicated and that financial information is more critical than ever."

"Yes, Matt. When you're talking about shrinking margins, increasing expenses, and facing new competitors, pennies can create your edge."

"Okay. Now, let's see if I still have any edge on this golf course," Matt said as he pulled out his driver and walked toward the tee box.

Twelfth Hole: You've Gotta Keep Score

1. *In business, sales, profits, sales productivity, inventory levels, cash, and accounts receivable are all part of the score. To be successful, you have to keep track of what you owe and what you own, how profitable you are, how much debt you have, and how much cash you have on hand.*
2. *Business owners must manage income statements to ensure profitability, balance sheets to manage assets and liabilities, and cash flow statements to ensure that there's enough cash on hand to meet obligations.*

Thirteenth Hole:

Even the Pros Have Pros

"My professional advce to you is to cheat."

Thirteenth Hole:
Even the Pros Have Pros

As Matt drove down the path they both looked at the beautiful raised tee box jutting out over the fairway next to them. "Since we've got a minute 'til the guys in front of us clear out, let me ask you about something you said a while ago that's been on my mind ever since. You said that training was the last thing that you would ever cut back on. My company is going through some difficult times, and I just can't spend much on training right now."

"Matt, that's about as big a mistake as you can make."

"But we don't have the budget for education—and our team doesn't have the time to take the training. They're too busy putting out fires!"

"What does that tell you?" Elizabeth asked.

"What?"

"That you're spending so much time putting out fires?"

"Uhhh …"

"It tells me that you're spending all your time focusing on what's going wrong and haven't properly trained your team to stay on the right course. The one thing that you have in your company, and that I have in mine, that should increase in value every day, is your team. If you're not giving them the proper training, you'll always have more fires to put out than you'll have opportunities to pursue," Elizabeth said.

"Where do you find the time? Your company is even busier than mine."

"Finding the time is not an issue. We understand the importance of providing training to our team. I just read in an article that the Container Store has been voted one of the top ten companies to work for in the United States for the last five years. We use them as a benchmark. When someone is hired to work at the Container Store, during their first year on the job, they receive something like 240 hours of training. Because they spend the time and the money to do this, their team members really are better than their competitors' teams. The results show up on their bottom line."

"We tried to give some training to our team a couple of years ago, Elizabeth, but everyone was always too busy to attend the sessions."

"And you let 'em get away with that?"

"I guess I did. We stopped having the training sessions a couple of months after they started."

"Matt, one of your challenges is that your team members probably look at training the way that I did after I graduated from college. The last thing I ever wanted to do was to attend another class. It took me several years to understand the importance of life-long learning.

"A friend gave me a series of training CDs on customer satisfaction. Remember my boring college experience? The last thing I wanted to do was to listen to a program about customer service. In the first place, I thought it would be mind numbing. Secondly, I thought we were already giving great service and didn't need to do much more. I considered myself a service expert. Since my friend spent quite a bit of money on the CDs, I decided that the least I could do was listen to them."

"And ..."

"Two things happened. First of all, I found them to be very interesting. I also found out that I didn't know everything that I needed to know about service. Many of the things on the audio CDs were common sense but were phrased in a way that I hadn't heard before. So, not only were the CDs entertaining and informative, but they actually gave me ideas that I was able to implement in our company. Our customers loved the changes—and our team members are having more fun than ever delivering great service. They are proud to be part of our team."

"It sounds like something I should do, but ..."

Elizabeth interrupted Matt, "But what? When we went from the back nine to the front nine, what did you see?"

"You mean the practice range?"

"Exactly! When the best golfers in the world finish a round of golf, many of them head straight to the range—with their trainers. In business, we have to be sure that our team members are well prepared. That means you have to find training materials that are educational—and interesting. You have to make sure that learning is a big part of every budget and that your team also budgets time for the programs. As they improve their skills, they will be energized, and they'll take their performance to the next level."

"I don't know, Elizabeth. My people aren't used to sitting through training programs. They may feel that it's a waste of their time."

"Only if they think *you* feel it's a waste. If you don't believe it will work, they'll pick that up in a heartbeat.

"We have less-formal learning also, Matt. I ask our best associates to mentor newer staff members and those who need a little help getting up to speed. Those asked to mentor their peers are honored and for the most part do a better job than I could ever do in helping their colleagues do better. Mentees appreciate the extra attention they get and the opportunity to improve their skills."

"So, I guess I've learned a couple of very important things on this hole."

"And what are those things, Matt?"

"I need to use business pros to coach my 'pros' how to do their jobs better and to spend the time and money on great training programs for my team members."

"Right."

Matt checked the fairway to make sure that the group in front of them was out of his way and then laced a gorgeous drive down the middle. He looked over at Elizabeth, who had that "I told you so" smile on her face.

"The coaching I'm getting from you today is invaluable," said Matt right after he swung. "Boy that felt good. I can't wait to see where my drive ended up. I've never hit a ball so well!"

Thirteenth Hole: Even the Pros Have Pros

1. *Training doesn't cost; it pays. Well-prepared associates are more productive, and their managers spend less time fighting fires.*

2. *Commit to lifelong learning. Subscribe and share industry journals; develop a schedule of training sessions; use outside presenters to keep meetings interesting; use fun audio and video clips and targeted PowerPoint presentations to keep sessions lively; develop a library of training DVDs, CDs, and Podcasts; involve associates in planning and presenting learning events.*

3. *Establish a mentoring program where team members can share their talents with their peers.*

4. *Evaluate staff performance to ensure that training mirrors your team's needs.*

Fourteenth Hole:

Why Players Have to Believe

"The easiest way to hook a ball is to try to slice it!"

Fourteenth Hole:
Why Players Have to Believe

Elizabeth hit her second shot into a sand trap next to the green. Matt had managed to reach the green in two shots. "I may finally win another hole," he said.

He watched as Elizabeth walked confidently into the sand trap, studied her lie, and then hit her shot just three feet from the hole. Matt took two putts to get his par, and Elizabeth managed to save her par with a three-foot putt.

As they rode to the next hole, Matt said, "That's the second time you've been in a sand trap today, and both times you hit great shots out of the sand. How do you do it?"

Trying not to gloat, Elizabeth said, "I used to hate sand traps too. Whenever I hit into one, I'd get flustered. Two things changed that."

Elizabeth went on, "Years ago, I read an article in a golf magazine about Tom Watson. He said something like 'the sand wedge made sand shots so easy it should be made an illegal club.' I thought to myself, 'Tom certainly has a positive attitude about this!'"

Matt smiled, "Yeah, he always looked pretty sure of himself."

"I realized that when I hit a shot into the sand, I was scared to death. It's like hearing that a major customer had lunch with your competitor. You might start thinking that you're about to lose the account. But if you're delivering your product and the service at a fair price, the odds are heavily in your favor that your client will continue to be loyal to you."

Matt agreed, "Fear can be pretty paralyzing."

"Then I wondered, 'What would it be like to walk into a sand trap with confidence like Tom Watson does?' I knew that a positive attitude had helped me be successful in business, and there was no reason sand traps should cause me such grief."

"You said that two things changed your attitude about being in the sand," Matt noted. "What's the second thing?"

"Having a positive attitude is essential, but it takes more than that. I realized that if I was going to be a better sand player, I'd have to do more than walk in a sand trap with a positive attitude. I'd definitely have to change the way I actually hit out of the sand."

"We'd all play better with more practice, Elizabeth," Matt said.

Elizabeth went on, "For the next couple of months, I read every article about getting out of the sand. These tips helped, but it took a lesson from my club pro, Mike, to develop the skill to actually give me confidence with my sand wedge."

"You've always said Mike was a terrific pro, Elizabeth."

"He is. He brought a piece of board to my lesson. At first, I wondered if he was going to hit me with the two-by-four when I made a bad shot!" Matt laughed as Elizabeth put her hands up in mock horror of being hit.

Elizabeth continued with her story. "Mike reached down and dug a small trench in the practice sand trap with his hand and then laid the board in the trench. Next he covered the board with about an inch of sand and set a golf ball on top of the sand. He then instructed me to hit the golf ball, making sure that my club reached down to the two-by-four as I made my swing."

"Did you hit the board?" Matt asked.

"No, but I thought to myself, 'This is crazy,' and gave it a try. The first four or five shots, I was afraid of hurting my wrists—or my club—by hitting the board. Mike kept encouraging me to make a swing so that I actually made contact with the board under the sand. It took several more attempts, but I was finally able to make the stroke that Mike was talking about. And the amazing thing was that my ball was flying out of the sand with ease. I started to focus on my target on the green and on making the right swing. It was great to watch my shots land close to the hole time and time again."

"It worked, huh?"

"It sure did, Matt. After using the board as a crutch, Mike moved me to another spot in the sand. He said, 'You can't take a two-by-four out on the golf course with you, so you need to have a mental image of that board an inch below the sand and making the same swing. Just hit an inch behind and an inch below your ball and you'll be just fine.'

"I was nervous trying to swing without that board. The first few attempts were very awkward, and the results weren't great. I flashed back to the positive attitude that Tom Watson has in sand traps and imagined that my board was still an inch below the sand. I spent the next half hour in that sand trap, and my skill improved with each swing."

Matt nodded. "Now you have skill and confidence."

"In golf, just like business, confidence plays a big part in being successful. You can't be consumed by what your competition is doing. To be successful in business, you have to be confident—in yourself and everyone in your company. But confidence isn't enough. You have to develop the skills that will help you overcome any obstacle," Elizabeth said.

"I guess I'm finding a few two-by-fours to use in getting my business back on track, Elizabeth. If we go back to our basics and get our team on board with our values, our mission, and our goals, they'll have the skills and the confidence to help us succeed."

Matt turned the cart toward the fifteenth tee box, thinking that he might go to Home Depot after his round to buy a two-by-four of his own.

Fourteenth Hole: Why Players Have to Believe

1. *A positive outlook can increase your ability to be successful. If you think you can sink a putt, make a sale, increase profits, or get a new customer, you're more likely to get it done than if you doubt you can do it.*
2. *Confidence and skill go hand in hand. You can't just will yourself to get out of a sand trap; you have to develop competence to match your confidence.*

Fifteenth Hole:

Why Business Is Only a Game

"You'll like our foursome. We take a mulligan on every hole, you get a free lift from water and sand traps. We don't count out of bounds and everything within five feet is a gimmee. Fred had a seventy-eight last week."

Fifteenth Hole:
Why Business is Only Game

Driving to the next tee box, Elizabeth asked, "Ever played with someone who was so serious about his golf that he couldn't have any fun?"

Matt nodded his head and smiled. "You mean like a guy who throws his club when he hits a bad shot?"

"Yeah. The kind of player who acts like he's got the Masters championship on the line with every putt."

"Playing with folks like that can sure ruin a round for me," Matt said. "They take all the enjoyment out of the game."

"Exactly. I mean I'm pretty competitive, and I like to win, but I want to have some fun when I come out."

"Me too. I guess some guys have a hard time drawing the line between passion and obsession. If you try to analyze every shot you make you never see the whole picture. You forget the how beautiful the course is, or the way the sun feels on your back, or the sounds of the geese in the lake. It's just about your score at the end of the day. And even if you beat yourself up you may not play any better the next time you go out."

Elizabeth nodded in agreement. "I've got a friend who's got the same problem in business. He's gone way past passionate. His approach to his company has actually made him sick from time to time."

"I know the type. They think if they put in twenty-hour days they'll move past their competitors. But instead, they usually burn out or lose their families in the process of chasing some dream."

"Even when things are as tough as they are for you now, Matt, I try to see my business as a bit of a game. I may need to take some lessons or improve my mental conditioning, but I try to ride out these cycles with some perspective."

"I guess when you have your money or your self-image or your confidence on the line it's easy to lose track of the real endgame," said Matt.

"Sure, and don't get me wrong—those things are important. But your business is what you do, not who you are. I think too many people—particularly entrepreneurs and executives—are a little mixed up about that."

"I guess some find it hard to keep their egos in check," Matt noted.

"I've got to work hard to keep some perspective. I have to back down sometimes and remind myself that my business is what I do to earn a living. It's what I do to provide for my family and to take care of my team members, my suppliers, my customers, and my community. If I make mistakes I may lose some money or have to dig out of some kind of hole, but it won't change who I am."

"You're so right, Elizabeth. I don't want to only be defined by the kind of business I run. I want my kids to think I'm the world's greatest dad and to have them learn about caring by the way I respect my associates. Sure I want my wife to be proud of me, but I want her to love me, too. And you've got to exhibit good sportsmanship in the marketplace, just like on the golf course."

"Right. Speaking of which ..." Elizabeth walked to her ball.

Fifteenth Hole: Why Business Is Only a Game

1. *Taking yourself—and your business—too seriously won't guarantee a better bottom line. Sometimes adding fun and joy can motivate you and your team to improve performance.*
2. *Business is what you do, not who you are. Happiness is rarely defined by the sales increases you attain, the new customer you land, or your title as owner or department manager.*

Sixteenth Hole:

Finding the Balance

"You're practicing your putting because you have a
golf match with your buddies in the morning!"

Sixteenth Hole:
Finding the Balance

When Matt put his ball on the tee, it fell off. He smiled and said, "I can't even get the ball to balance on the tee; much less balance all the stuff in my life." Matt put the ball back on the tee and hit it into a fairway bunker.

"I don't get it, Elizabeth. You are very successful in your work, but I know that you somehow find the time to spend time with your family, you're involved in a couple of charities—and you certainly find more time to play golf than I do!"

"Balance is something that I've struggled with, Matt. I actually got two different points of view from my dad that really confused me, and it's taken some time to work through my balance issues."

"How did your dad confuse you?"

"Well, about the time that I started my company, Dad and Mom came to visit. One night, Dad and I were alone in the living room. He told me that he was excited about the new direction I was taking and then became quite reflective."

"'Elizabeth,' Dad said, 'I worked for Chandler Distributors for thirty years. I started in sales and worked my way up to the top 10 percent of all the salespeople in the organization. I was better than 90 percent of all the other salespeople.

"'Eventually, they put me in a management role. They gave me the worst sales team in the entire organization, and in just two years, my group moved to the top 10 percent of all teams at Chandler, and we stayed in the top 10 percent until I retired. We were better than 90 percent of the other sales teams in the company.'

"But then he told me this: 'Elizabeth, I'm retired now, and I look back at the success I had in my working years. The top 10 percent is pretty darn good ...'"

Elizabeth put her thumb and first finger about a half inch apart and said, "But I wonder what would have happened if I had just tried this much harder."

Matt said, "I don't see anything confusing about that, Elizabeth. He was telling you that you need to work just a little bit harder than you think you do."

"I'm not finished with the story, Matt. After listening to my dad talk about working harder, I probably worked too much for the next few years. Then my dad surprised me."

"How?"

"Several years after our 'work harder' conversation I sat down with him to record his answers to some questions I asked him about his life. He had been retired for about five years, and during the taped sessions, he said something that blew me away."

"What was that?"

"'Elizabeth,' Dad told me, 'I sometimes wonder if I would have been better off if I'd just had a nine-to-five job, like at the post office, and had been able to just come home and leave work behind each day.'"

Matt waved at the ranger they passed as he drove toward the fairway, "Yeah, I can see how that confused you, Elizabeth. After hearing the 'work harder' speech, it must have really made you wonder what he really believed."

"You're right. This was totally out of the blue. After working so hard since Dad's 'work harder' speech, I realized that I had to find the balance between 'work harder' and 'nine to five.'"

"So, what did you do?"

"It took some time to work out, Matt. I had been so focused on working harder. I began to see that I wasn't spending enough time with my family. I was also letting lots of other things go, too, like golf.

"Matt, I knew that I didn't want to sell my company and go to work for the post office, but I realized that I had to adjust my priorities. I sat down and talked with my family about ways that we could spend more time together—quality time. I read an article about time management and slowly rearranged my schedule. It's been so much better the past couple of years."

"Like I said before, I'm working eighty hours a week, Elizabeth, and I don't seem to be getting anything done now. How can I possibly work fewer hours?"

"You have to work smarter. It's not about working longer hours. Talk to your family and figure out how you can spend more quality time with them. Sit down and prioritize what is important to you, and decide where you're spinning your wheels. You'll find a new sense of energy and will be far more productive.

"Look around the golf course today, Matt. It's a weekday, and yet the course is full of people. I'll bet that many of them took the afternoon off to play golf. They could be at work, but they're balancing their lives with a round of golf today. I sometimes think it's better to be golfing, even if I feel guilty that I'm not at work, than to be at work, wishing I were golfing."

"You're right, Elizabeth. I'm working way too many hours and not having much fun. I haven't made it to my softball league games all season. It's time to balance things in my life."

"Matt, it will take some time to adjust, but your family will be happy that you did it—and so will you."

"Now, let's see if we can balance our scorecards a little better. We could both use a couple of pars."

Sixteenth Hole: Finding the Balance

1. *Work-life balance creates a better business climate, more energized team members, and more enthusiastic managers. Some companies have found that offering extended family leave and even sabbaticals has reduced turnover and improved productivity.*
2. *Making time to participate in community activities, spending time with family, and developing hobbies motivates owners and staff members to work up to their potential when they are on the job.*

Seventeenth Hole:

How Leadership Drives Success

"I'm playing golf this afternoon, Smith.
Do something about this rain."

Seventeenth Hole:
How Leadership Drives Success

As he walked off the green Matt said, "There's something else I struggle with, Elizabeth."

"What's that?"

"The whole notion of leadership. I mean I've been in my business a long time. I've done practically every job in the company. I can still sell our products to anyone. I could fill in for almost anyone and do a pretty good job."

"That doesn't sound like a bad thing, Matt."

"It's just that now that I'm at the top, I'm not sure exactly what my job is. I've always been a good self-starter, but I don't seem to be growing as fast as my responsibilities are."

"I think that's a big problem for most entrepreneurs. We start our businesses because of a passion or because someone opened up an opportunity to us and we didn't really have a manual about how to get things done."

Matt chuckled, "It's sort of how I felt when I first had kids, I guess."

"Sure. It's not too different. It's old fashioned on-the-job training."

"Sometimes I feel like the only way to get things done right is to do them myself. I know that's not great management, but I still tend to do things the way I did when the company was a lot smaller and I had my fingers in everything."

"You're a sports fan, right?"

"Yep."

"Well, try to see your role like that of the coach of a team. You don't see coaches going out to make the big plays when the team's behind or when the star shooter gets injured do you?"

"No. But ...,"

"Well, real leadership is sharing responsibilities and letting others take ownership of their challenges and find their own solutions. I worked in my dad's shop for a while in college. My grandmother was insistent that I count the cash drawer exactly like she did. Pennies, nickels, dimes, quarters, ones, fives, tens, etc. Of course I was defiant of any authority and counted the twenties, the tens, the fives ... and she went ballistic. She was convinced I'd never be able to make a $200 drawer unless I did it her way. It wasn't good leadership, and I didn't get the point she was trying to make. She wasn't a good coach. You have to learn to stay on the bench and let your players win the game for you. As a leader, you've got to strategize the big plays and debrief the game films."

"Maybe you're right, Elizabeth. I had a great golf coach in high school. He was really charismatic, so everyone wanted to be on the golf team. He hadn't played competitively himself in years, but we won the state championship my senior year."

"What were his secrets, Matt?"

"Well, he made everyone feel important. We were taught that everyone on our team was key to winning, and we learned great respect for kids who weren't terrific golfers."

"Wouldn't those things work in your business?"

"Sure. I remember something else he did. He enforced his rules—things like not missing practice—by talking to us one on one. He never singled a guy out in front of the others."

"Okay. What else did you learn from your coach?"

"He helped us set goals. Some were short term, like how long we'd spend on the practice range or on the putting green or how to win the next match, but he also helped us see the big picture. He'd count down for us—two more wins and we'd take the city title; win four matches in the playoffs and we'd get to state. Once we got there we'd know just what we'd have to do to win the title."

"Goal setting is a great life skill isn't it, Matt?"

"Yep. I think I also learned personal responsibility on that team. We weren't a big school. Nearly every kid played some sport. We didn't have a big golf team, so we needed everyone to show up, to be committed, to work hard, and to act like a winner."

"Kind of like in your company, right?"

"Yeah, I really need everyone to pull together to get our business turned around. I need a full team, I guess."

"There's something else I've learned, Matt. There's a difference between management and leadership. You *manage* things—like inventory and accounts receivable—but you *lead* people."

"That makes sense. We had a great captain on our team. He helped with our gear and made sure we wore the right shirts, but he didn't run our practices. Coach did that."

"You could lead your managers differently too, Matt. Each manager may also have people that they have to lead, but they have to manage things like sales growth, cash flow, and traffic. Part of your job is to help them see the difference and to develop skills for both."

"There's another thing, Elizabeth. We had to try out for the team every year. Being a good player never guaranteed you a spot the next year. I can't have my associates apply for their jobs every year, but I guess regular performance reviews would be helpful to my staff and would help me understand their strengths and weaknesses better. They'd have a better chance of succeeding, and I'd probably have more people doing the things they're really good at."

"You probably would."

"And I guess I have to realize that some of my team members are just never going to help me win our matches. Maybe some other staffers would be better playing in different positions or even on other teams."

"It sounds like your coach taught you a lot about leadership. Now you just have to put on your coaching cap and get back to the basics, Matt."

Matt nodded and drove to the next tee box.

Seventeenth Hole: How Leadership Drives Success

1. *Management and leadership are different; you manage things—like cash, inventory, and receivables—but you lead people.*
2. *As a coach, your job is to encourage personal responsibility, enforce rules fairly, and make everyone feel like an important member of the team.*
3. *Lead by example to help managers become leaders themselves. Coach them to improve the way they interact with their team members. Compliment them when they do a great job to reinforce their behavior.*
4. *Great coaches give regular performance reviews to help team members know their strengths and weaknesses so they can improve their games.*

Eighteenth Hole:

One Is the Loneliest Number

©Bob Zahn

"I thought you were going to have <u>me</u> up and swinging, doc?"

Eighteenth Hole:
One is the Loneliest Number

As they approached the eighteenth tee, Matt said, "Elizabeth, with all the things I've learned from you today, I'm going to go back and bury my competitors."

"Matt, competition is a good thing."

"What? Are you kidding?"

"No, competition keeps you sharp. On top of that, I learn a lot from other people in my industry."

"How do you do that? Don't they just want you to go away?"

"On the contrary, Matt. I'm a member of our industry's trade association, and getting together with others in the business is good for us all."

"Our company belongs to an association too, but all we do is send in our dues so that we can take advantage of their discounted insurance programs."

"It's great to get your insurance through your association, but you're missing a lot of value that your association probably offers you.

"Golf, for example, has the PGA tour for the male pros, the LPGA for the female pros, and the USGA for the amateur golfers. Like golfers, every business owner should be active in their trade association."

"Why?"

"Every trade association is different, but there are four main benefits that I receive from belonging to mine. Since you've already mentioned it, I'll start with the savings I get on insurance and many other things, like discounts on car rental and office supplies.

"Second, my industry has several challenges with legislative issues. In fact, when you talk about competition, the government probably affects my bottom line more than anyone! I have to have a voice in our state and national legislatures, and I can't do it by myself. My association is terrific when it comes to keeping me up-to-date on the issues that may affect me and lets me know when they need my help in contacting my representatives at the state capital—or in Washington."

"I guess it does make sense to have a collective voice with the legislators," Matt said.

"Makes sense? It's a no-brainer, Matt. With the help of the other companies in your industry, your friendly competitors, you can be proactive on the issues that affect your industry."

"What else do you get from your association?"

"Education. My association sponsors several educational events every year, including a national convention. At these meetings, industry experts and top-notch professional speakers share their expertise. I go to as many of these as possible and bring my team members with me too."

"And what's the fourth benefit?"

"Networking. You talk about your competition in lots of negative ways. For me, my competitors aren't my enemies. I feel that we're all in business together, and we can help each other become more successful.

"Sure, if I'm with a local competitor, there are some things that I might not share. But on general business strategies, we do find lots of common ideas that can benefit everyone. I have great relationships with people I've met at the national association meetings. We've formed a peer review group to benchmark our businesses. We even share our financial results."

"You're kidding!"

"No, there's great value in sharing these numbers with people who have a business in the same industry as mine. It's 'apples to apples.' It helps me measure myself with my peers and shows me where I can improve my bottom line."

"You really do believe in associations, but I've always been taught to stay away from my competitors. I'm still not convinced, though, but maybe I'll try going to a local chapter meeting."

Matt put his ball on the tee and ripped a beautiful drive down the middle of the fairway.

"There are lots of other reasons to join an association." Elizabeth laughed out loud and said, "Here's the best part, Matt. Most associations have at least one golf tournament for their members every year."

"Where do I sign up?" Matt laughed back.

Eighteenth Hole: One Is the Loneliest Number

1. *Trade associations are important business tools. They lobby on issues common to their members and provide networking and learning opportunities and money-saving services. You can find listings of local and national trade groups on the Internet.*
2. *Talk to other members to see how they value the association; attend a few meetings as a guest.*

Nineteenth Hole:

Putting It All Together

Alex's golf scores improved greatly after he joined the Liar's Club.

Nineteenth Hole:
Putting It All Together

As they headed into the clubhouse, Matt reflected on the lessons that he had learned from Elizabeth during their round. He was feeling renewed by the time they had spent together. In fact, he had more energy than he did when they teed off on the first hole a few hours before. Instead of dreading going into work the next day, he was already excited about it.

Matt and Elizabeth both smiled when the waitress came to take their drink order. "Can I get you a couple of beers?" she asked.

Matt answered, "Sure. I'll have a Heineken. Elizabeth?"

"I'll have an Arnold Palmer please," she said as she totaled up their score cards.

"You were right, Elizabeth."

"About what?"

"About the business lessons you can find on a golf course. I think I've been like most businesspeople out there. I've been running my business the way I think my competitors run theirs. If someone else brought in a new line, I got a similar one. When someone else started a new marketing program, I answered it. If I heard that a competitor gave his team members a bonus, I thought I had to give mine one too.

"I've spent most of the last nineteen years following others instead of leading my own pack. Our business does have strengths. There are lots of things we do better than anyone else. I just haven't been focused on improving our game as much as I need to. I'm so worried about what my competitors are doing with their companies that I don't have time to manage mine."

"Sounds like you've learned some tough lessons along the way, Matt."

"Maybe not as well as I should have, though. But from now on, I'm going to concentrate on our business and run it like a pro."

"And how are you going to that, Matt?"

"Well, first I'm going to try to figure out where we're going. I'm going to define a clear vision. I want to really be able to see what success looks like. Kind of like seeing the ball go right into the cup as you tee off on a long par three. Or like you did when you filled in your scorecard before we even teed off."

"That's a good place to start."

"I'm going to pay a lot more attention to the kind of experience our customers get. I don't want customer service to be some sort of empty promise. I want my customers to know how important they are and how much we care about them *and* their businesses. We're not going to settle for having a crew of order takers. My team is going to be made up of true sales professionals. Everyone in the company is going to learn to be an ambassador of our service commitment.

"I'm going to look at some real performance metrics and share more financial information with my staff. We're going to become a learning organization as well. I can't afford not to train my people if I want them to excel.

"And we're going to pay attention to our branding. If we continue to act like we're just another company selling commodity products, that's all we'll ever be. But if our brand is tied to our service, the community we live in, and the people who work with us, we'll differentiate ourselves from the others in the industry."

"I think you're getting it, Matt."

"Yeah, and I know that no matter how hard we try to avoid them we'll run into roadblocks along the way, but we'll deal with those hazards with good business practices and by developing the skills to get out of trouble when it does happen."

Elizabeth nodded as she said, "You sound a lot more confident than you did a few hours ago, Matt."

"But at the same time, I want to try to remember that my business isn't my whole life. It's not who I am. My friends and my family have been through a lot with me lately, and I need to find some balance so that I can give something back to them.

"And I want to be a better leader. I want to develop my team and communicate regularly and openly with them. I want them to feel like I'm open to their ideas and that I value their input.

"I feel better, too, Elizabeth. I know I'm good enough to win this game. I can't believe I let my business get to this point, but I know I can pull it out. I've got a lot of folks counting on me, and I don't want to disappoint them."

"That's all great stuff, Matt, but don't try to do too much at once. You'll get overwhelmed and just give up. What are the two or three things we talked about today that you think will have the biggest and most immediate impact?"

"Hmmmm. That's tough, but I think you're right," Matt said thoughtfully.

"So, where are you going to get the biggest bang?" Elizabeth asked.

"Well," Matt said, "I've got to be a better coach to create a winning team. I've got to be a better leader. I've got to quit moaning and start setting a positive example to get some new things done."

"That's good; what else?"

"I guess it would be understanding that risk taking and managing change are part of business. Just like the conditions on the golf course will change from day to day, today's business environment is also fluid. It doesn't make sense to stand still and hope things settle down. I've got to take a certain amount of calculated risk to stay ahead of the curve. I can't ignore what's happening around us." Matt said.

"Wow, Matt. I think that's all great, but there's one more thing."

"What's that?"

"You didn't even ask me how you scored today. Even though you haven't played much you still shot an eighty-four."

"That's great, Elizabeth, but the real win lies ahead when I put some of your great ideas to use in my business."

"They're not all my ideas, but they're lessons I've learned along the way in my own business. I'm glad to help."

Lessons from the Links

"Let's play again next month, Elizabeth. I'll spend some time on the practice range between now and then. And I know I'll have some good news to report about my business."

"It's a date."

Matt not only learned a lot about business that day, but he learned about himself. He learned that the success of his business was *his* job and that his competitors weren't going to make him better or worse.

Elizabeth helped Matt see what success would look like and to set meaningful goals and measures.

Matt realized that he had to have the right team in place and to lead and coach them. They needed support, training, achievable goals, and to feel like part of the company's winning formula.

No matter how great his products and services were, Matt's customers needed—and deserved—a great buying experience. His team had to act like professional sales consultants, not like order takers.

His company brand was a promise of quality and service to his customers, and Matt had to deliver on that promise. And he was reminded of the importance of business ethics—no matter how tough business gets, or how stiff the competition is, you have to play by the rules.

He learned that although he does need to have the right equipment and technology, he can't buy his way into sales growth, profitability, and success.

Like golf, business has hazards. There are unhappy customers, cash shortages, and inventory imbalances. Knowing how to get through these obstacles is critical to effective management.

The scorecard in business includes the income statement, balance sheet, and cash flow projections as well as metrics on sales, margin, productivity, and asset management. Business leaders can develop dashboards to quickly view the important numbers regularly.

Elizabeth taught Matt the importance of allowing his company to become a learning organization and making a commitment to continually upgrading his team.

Most of all, Matt was forced to see that running his business is what he does, not who he is. He can lead it and make it successful, but that's not the only measure of his personal worth.

Matt probably knew most of what he and Elizabeth talked about long before he called for her advice. The big lesson may be that he just needed someone to help him regain confidence in his game. He was paralyzed by his fear and his competition.

After a round of golf, Matt was energized and enthusiastic about his ability to turn his company around.

Elizabeth knew she'd have a fierce new competitor the next time she and Matt went out to play.

To contact Elly Valas or to order copies of Guerrilla Retailing send a message to elly@ellyvalas.com

To contact Mark Mayberry or to order copies of Building a Dream Workforce send a message to mark@markmayberry.com

About the Authors

Elly Valas is a small-business consultant, speaker, and writer. She is the author of *Guerrilla Retailing.* She lives in Denver and is a high-handicap duffer hoping to score under her weight.

Mark Mayberry is a professional speaker and the author of *Building a Dream Workforce.* He is an avid golfer and lives in Rockford, Illinois.